Mind Chronicles

the Safest Place is Created

Melissa Calixte

Foreword

A poignant insight of a new author on the rise. She shares her thoughts and views of nature and of life itself. Her observations and metaphors will speak volumes to you…- Rita

To the people who have helped me from near or far, sometimes without even knowing it. May God bless you! You have been part of my edification, whether by creation or destruction. -Mel

Content

1

Timeless

Please stay right here in my mind, my head, my soul.
Help me redefine this notebook.
Let these feelings wash over me relentlessly.
May these words be timeless and
This world, this perpetual myth of paradise…

2

Release

Shut up! Be quiet.
Let me have my peace.
You are too loud.
I want you to stay silent and give me a break here.
Release me so I can start over.
Just don't bring me back, where I don't belong anymore.

No

No, I say no!

I do not want that!

Get out of there!

I do not believe it!

I don't want you!

I am not that one!

It is not me!

I am just being me.

Breathe

I don't know who I am anymore
I don't know how to feel anymore
I don't know how to write anymore
How to be
How to breathe
And how to think about being right here

Emptiness

I need a place to wash and empty my mind
Somewhere I can connect with another world
Another existence
Where the pressure could go away
I need to purify myself
And to be me
Another kind of me

Shame

It's a shame,
These feelings.
Why are you here?
What do you want?
Why are you inside of my heart?
I can't stand you.
Because of you I feel bad.
I feel sad.
I feel ungrateful.
It's a disgrace to what God brought into my life.

Ugly

I can be pretty.
I can be ugly.
I can sketch a smiley face
or show no pity.
One day, I might understand.
The other, I'll warn you to stop.
You better stop!
Oh, I can be very ugly.

Mad

I am mad at myself.
I am not able to control these emotions.

I am mad at myself.
I am not grateful enough.

I am mad at myself.
I hate what I can't control.

I am mad at myself.
Relying only on positivity is making me so vulnerable.

I hate it.
But I love and accept who I am.
These feelings are part of me.

Exhaustion

I am tired.
My mind is tired.
My soul is tired.
My body is tired of hiding it.
It's too much effort.

I lost myself.
I lost my purpose.
What I am feeling are the collateral damages.
I am keeping this from me.
This person has to come out!

Now, I am finally here.
The truth has been revealed.
It's time to get it out.
I will unravel this gift and I will catch up
With Time and invalidate this imposter.

Is this the end?

I don't believe it;
My heart is overfilled with hope.
Is this the end?
I don't believe it;
Joy takes all over my tears.
Is this the end?
Impossible, my hope and savior
Are giving me the wisdom and the courage.
I will give it a chance to heal the world
Before the final call home.

The best way

Not only we live in a world,

Where chaos and hatred

Seem to be louder than love and empathy;

But we live in a world where we are judged

On how strong we stand in front of them.

We all do it in some kind of way.

Somehow, it seems that there is a "best" way of doing it;

A "best" way of yelling how hurt we are;

A "best" way to cry for help;

A "best" way to protest about things that hurt humanity;

A "best" way to live in harmony with our emotions;

A "best" way to breathe.

But what is the "best" way to expose silence

As the king of all evil?

12

Speak up

What will make this world a better place?
A better you?
A better me?
A better us?
Does it have to change?
What is a change?
What is "better"?
What is unacceptable?
What is?
How to discuss what's on your mind?
Speak up for you, for everyone!
What are the changes you want to see in the world?
And what are the benefits?
What are the benefits for yourself and the people around you?
Is this going to change the world?

It definitely has to change somehow.

Strong

Anything trying to break you won't work.

You are stronger than this.

Anything trying to make you pay for the life you chose for yourself won't work.

You are stronger than this.

Other people's behavior will never win if the purpose is to destroy you.

You are stronger than their worst opponent.

Wish them to learn how to love.

Wish them to learn how to respect their true selves.

Wish them to win their battle to self-love.

THEY must be stronger than this!

Failure

I think I love to fail.
Something about failure
Is tremendously powerful.
Something about failure
Can reveal so many things,
So many sides,
And so many stories.
But I guess I just have to learn
To stand back up, though.

Admirer

Who do you think you are?

I dare you to challenge me!

I dare you to stand in my way!

I dare you to try to put the brakes on my plans!

Who do you think you are?

Who do you think you are?

Are you my enemy, my friend, my greatest admirer?

Who do you think you are?

I can't believe you standing here trying to change my ways, my plans my dreams.

I believe that I am this great admirer, this friend and this enemy.

I am the only one standing in my way.

Slave

I am no longer a slave.
I am no longer a slave of this world.
I refuse to be imprisoned and to suffocate.
These people have learned to remain in chains.

They couldn't show me to free myself.
They are a prisoner, a prisoner of misfortune of sadness;
Of the misery of being themselves.

They haven't learned to love.
I can't show it to them.
Can I?

All I know is how to free myself from slavery.
I have learned how to love
And it set me free.

Free my mind

Is my mind completely empty?
It feels like there's nothing in here.

How do I get my pen to do its job
When my heart can't even disentangle what is from what was?

No... My heart has its reasons.
My reason knows nothing about it.
I don't need that reason!

Secret waves

The waves make it perfectly clear
"Follow the lead"
They say

I can hear it, the silent noise
The future is somewhere working
And revamping a new world
A new era
A new sun

Listen to the wind whispering in your ear
The secret of this Brand-New Day

The beauty in gray

Here comes the rain;

Here comes the thunder;

Here come the other aspects of beauty.

What do I know about the rain?

The sun rises right after…

Language

I can't ignore the signs.
Your message is crystal clear.
There must be something we can do.
This part of my brain is reacting and craving attention.
Your language,
You win.
Tell me now, where do we stand today?

Little bits

A little bit of you
To heal the world

A little bit of you
To light up the darkest skies

A little bit of you
To bring joy and happiness to the most hopeless hearts

A little bit of you
To share this passion
And make the earth turn the other way

I believe you do make a difference
The power you bring in this world
Has a meaning nobody else can ever reveal

All I need is just a little bit of you

Judgmental

No one can stand there and judge me.
I am safe behind this pen.
No one can stand there and judge me.
I am safe behind these creations.

God got me.

I am the master of my mind
And of my thoughts and feelings.
I have all the right to do as it pleases me.
This pen is my weapon.
This head is my safe place.

God is my solace.

When I close my eyes

I see little bits of my life
When I close my eyes;
Little bits of my life overlapping.

All events take on their full meaning.
I try to hold onto my reality.
I refuse to accept them.

A nightmare and a beautiful dream,
That's what it is.
I close my eyes again.

The call

Classical music resonates and calls out to me.
Nature constantly whispers to join her.
I don't recognize this person.

I don't recognize her.
I'm afraid to go to her.
Should I go to her?

Why are there so many emotions?
Why are musical instruments giving me a message?

They open their soul and it is impossible to communicate.
I once refused to open myself to it.

I don't know how to read or interpret it;
Let alone play it.
Is it too late to join the family?

Peace

That's all I need.
That's all I want.
That's all would help me
To find everything to be me.

When I listen to the wind,
I know that there is somewhere I'd rather be.
Somewhere I can feel and taste;
Somewhere I can find the resilience to fight the rest.

Give me a moment of silence.
Give me hope.
Give me a little bit of me.
Give me this silent moment to be me.

Solace

I remember grandma walking around, outside.
She was making sure I was ok.
I remember her standing there.

I was crying.
I didn't want to be there with these educators asking me
to play with the other kids.

I didn't want to play.
I wanted to go back home and be with her.
But I had to stay and play.

She was there anyway.
She was walking around the corner.
and watching over me.

I could see her through the window.
"Grandma is still here."
"Everything will be okay" little me.

I was not at all comfortable
but somehow, I found solace.

Rainy night

Here comes the rain again,
I can hear a pretty noise.
Oh, my beautiful rainy night!
You are my divine soothing sound.

May the lapping of these raindrops,
Be incredibly miraculous
And a real medicine for my ears.
They have suffered long enough.

Let this water operate.
Oh, my beautiful rainy night!
I need you; I love you,
I can hear you.

Winter sunrise

Here, on my bed with a pen and a notebook,
I am looking at the candle burning.
There is absolutely no noise.
I can finally write.

No talking, no crying;
Only the music of a pure warm heart.
I wish I could freeze this moment.
I pray the clock to stop and enjoy it forever.

Please, Tomorrow stay away.
I need one more moment, one more heartbeat.
Can I breathe this and be still?
I want to play around with freedom

And cuddle with this magnificent scent of purity.
Let me just fall in love with the winter sunrise
Coming right on time.

Dear hope

Give me back my brain.
I can't think anymore.
Give me back my soul.
I can't see what used to push me through.
But I still have my heart beating fast enough,
And my spirit is reconnecting.
Thank God, my hands are writing.
Dear hope, I knew you were there.

Ready

I stand here still, hoping.
I sit here still wishing.
I am fixing this flame and praying for redemption.

This world is completely insane, sometimes brainless.
My heart is heavy and my spirit is tired.

But here comes the best of me,
Ready to overcome anything.

Brand new day

Hope of a brand-new day
Hope of a brand-new world
Hope of brand-new colors

My heart is full of these great moments,
When I used to play outside,
Nothing else in my mind but joy and laughter.

Birds are singing, kids are playing.
Wow! The neighbor, Miss Johns, she is baking cookies.

My nose is grateful for this delightful instant,
Pure happiness as authentic feelings.
Hope of a brand-new day

Sunny days

The sun is kissing my skin.
Anything for this feeling.
May my soul be my currency,
To be one with these powerful sparkles.
It is my only wish.
I do believe in paradise.
It's right here, right now.
I am blind to think I deserve a place in heave.
It is already there.
Kiss me good night
To the moon and back.
I am ready for you in the morning,
Where I belong.
Envelop me in your warmth and tenderness.
Sunny days are here to stay.

True colors

The leaves decide to show their best colors before dying.
They fight until the end;
But as they believe in the beauty of the last dance;
They come back for another season.

Spring will come back.
The flowers will bloom again.
Fall is finally here.
The sun is shining through.

The colors are reflecting this intense sense of purity.
This new season is a true deliverance.
This time around, are they here to stay?

My beauties will find the way to dance for a very moment;
In this new colorful wardrobe;
Alongside the wind, the rain and my soul.
As the sun comes up, they will meet again.

Intuitive

It's all about embracing the unknown,

Trusting your instinct and that little voice telling you the truth.

It's also about faith;

Kissing destiny and opening the path to freedom.

Water, dear water

How can I explain this?

You are beautiful beyond words.

In your arms, I find comfort.

You never let me fall and you listened to every tear.

I know this stays between us.

Only the sunlight,

Only the sunlight as a witness.

Lamentations of the heart

What if I suddenly realize, my life was worth living.
Will I get another chance to make it work this time?
I deserve to know the true meaning behind my existence.
I deserve to discover what will make my heart smile.
I have got to have another chance.
I will… I will.
But what am I going to do with it?
Tell me.
I need a sign… I need a sign.
What happens after the spark?

Still

This flame is completely consumed.
I need to bring it back.
Well, if there is any spark left.
Just be there and light up what I still have.
The remaining piece of my soul
Is still there waiting to execute the mission.
Both parts of me,
The one that ran away
And she who is ready to fight,
Are responding and waiting for you.

Raindrops

Somewhere behind these curtains,
I can hear the raindrops.
There is nothing more to change.

What could be more elegant
Than the sound running down the river?
All these water droplets;
Deep sorrow or eternal happiness?

The sun comes up.
Spring has become the hero.
The sun is here.
Your smile is ready to shine through these curtains.

Do you hear the raindrops?

Blazing fire

My heart has been pounding long enough
To keep decent energy.

It is now time to take the lead
And remind my body functions
You are everything they need.

Will it burn still?
Let me strike back that fire and never let it die.

Anything

You are ready to do anything
To get there
Unexpected things happen and you go off the rails
It's not easy when your standards are so high
That even you can't reach
Or are they already?
How do you cope when others can't match
This picture you created in your mind
For them to fit in?
Nobody fits in.
I don't fit in.
No one should anyway
Because it just wasn't meant to be
These are not the rules of life
What are the rules?
There are absolutely none!

Love of my life

I am chasing you.
I am chasing authenticity.
I am chasing a heartbeat.
It's in there, it's in there;
Deeper, deeper.

All in me

Love is what I see.
Love is what I feel.
Love is what I imagine.

It's what I share.
But it's also what I expect,
What I dream of
And what I want to breathe.

That kind is nothing
Someone can offer me.
There is no one but me in here.
It is all in me.

Here

Here, it is here
This color, this warmth, this smell
It's here
Unforgettable moments and insane desires
It's here
The dreams of tomorrow and the pleasures of today
It's here
I only think of you and this real hope that one day
It will be here
Step out of the clouds until the sun shines

Paradise

Use your sight to tell your soul where to go.
It smiles and shouts to the devil to let go.
The game is over.
Here is paradise.

Free

Writing is freedom!
No one judges the paintings of an artist.
No one condemns the colors and the upside-down shapes
All over the place.
No one judges the meaning of thoughts.
You are free to be anything you want.

Home

Emotions are my driving essence.

If I can't connect anymore,
I might as well be dead.

Following miserably by selling my soul,
I might as well be the devil.

Not living as I believe with freedom and authenticity,
I might as well be a prisoner.

But I live to feel and my mind and soul
Are completely listening to my environment.

I might as well find my place called home.

Sweet pleasures

Are music and language stored in the same part of the brain?

I have always wondered
Where these sweet pleasures come from;
These moments of pure happiness
And these enchanting countries.

I have dreams of this world
Where sounds love to dance with the melodies
Of the kingdom I would create.

I don't know in which part of my brain
You're hiding, dear talent
But it's time to wake up.

With the time passing by,
The clock keeps running
And my life will then be erased;

Let me leave a trace.

Eternity

Sweet beauty,
Watching you makes me realize,
How I wish you were eternal.
But what does eternity look like?

Your beauty is rich.
You reassure me.
It wouldn't be fair.
What's eternal does not have this essence.
Well, I don't know.

I know I enjoy taking care of you;
Knowing that you won't always have that glow.
Your beauty will fade,
But your presence right now is one of the most beautiful creations.

I can't help but think of
How lucky I am to be able to look at you.
Sweet beauty…
But what does eternity look like?

She only needs me

I could admire her relentlessly;
So wonderful, so strong, so beautiful,
So fragrant and radiant.

Her warmth is reassuring
But also frightening.

Unique and delicate marvel,
I wish she could stay forever.
She will eventually weaken and die out.

What does she need?
What does she need?

I think she only needs me.

Healing

No, this is a complete lie!
The earth hasn't stopped.
In fact, she is more than fine.

You just gave her a break!
Life is right there.
You can't see it because you have been distant.
For far too long, you've been living in this fake environment.
Your behavior kept you from your natural birth rights.

Just wake up for a minute.
Why are you doing this?
Wake up!
Stand outside and breathe.
Breathe from all your lungs.

Stand still and take a look at the movements.
The trees are smiling,
The wind is talking to the leaves
And the birds are singing, free.
They are free!

Stand still and you should now understand,
Why the wind has always been so strong.
Stand still and listen to the silence of mother nature,
Telling you that she is healing.
And let her show you, how you could too.

Brain full motion

All this complex brain as a gift, all for myself?
I say thank you.

I want to show my multiple me now.
I want to show all my talents and be her at the same time.

I want to be everything I one day decided to ignore.
The world shut the doors.

The world keeps shutting them
By telling me to choose
And to stay on my field, my lane.

Which lane are you talking about, world?
I am picking up everything I like.

Dare to stop me!

Picture perfect

My heart burns with desires for a new era
Where my body, soul, mind and dreams are one.
As for my eyes,
They can only contemplate the life I will create;
As I build a legacy that will last forever.

Something you dream of

Sweet insane perfume
Breath of life and intense thoughts
Obsessive need to pick you up
And admire you
Hope and create this image
To finally welcome
What is destiny for me

Smile

Any reason to smile is something you should carefully cherish;
Any reason to smile is one more hopeful way to reach for the stars;
Any reason to smile is the light through your darkest moments;
Any reason to smile is God's message that everything is handled;
Any reason to smile is yours, truly...

Be you

Dear younger self,
I know what it is to be different.
I know what it is to be out of the box,
Out of the team, the league,
Out of the minds.
But don't be afraid.
Just take advantage of it.
It's yours, it's your gift, your divine success.
Don't be afraid to show your colors.
Don't be afraid, don't be afraid.
You're different, but it's you, right?
Yes, you are different.
But you get to be who you are.

Loyalty

My intuition, my friend, my loyal half;
My natural spirit and divine access;

Thank you for your guidance and for opening the doors of faith,
When my mind steps to shut all possibilities.

I have learned to use you, to understand
And to follow you.

May you be there in every step of the way,
Until the very end.

To you

I don't know if you can feel this,
But I know you can definitely read my words.
With everything I have inside,
I can hear your heartbeat searching for the way to grab this shining star.
It only takes courage and a little bit of your soul.
Don't think.
Just stand still, stay here, be quiet.
Inhale and exhale your entire being into this image of you.
Please just give yourself one chance to live.

Éternité (French original)

Douce beauté,
Te regarder me fait réaliser,
À quel point j'aimerais que tu sois éternelle.
Mais à quoi ressemble l'éternité?
Ta beauté est riche, éclatante et tu me rassures.
Ce ne serait pas juste.
Ce qui est éternel n'a pas cette essence.
Du moins, je ne sais pas.
Je sais que j'ai plaisir à prendre soin de toi,
Sachant que tu n'auras pas toujours cet éclat.
Ta beauté se fanera
Mais ta présence en ce moment est l'une des plus belles créations.
Je ne peux m'empêcher de penser
À la chance que j'ai de pouvoir te regarder.
Douce beauté...
Mais à quoi donc ressemble l'éternité?

Non

Non, je dis non!

Je ne veux pas!

Pousse-toi de là!

Je n'y crois pas!

Je ne te veux pas!

Je ne suis pas celle-là!

Ce n'est pas moi!

Je ne suis que moi.

Que de moi

Je pourrais admirer cette flamme sans relâche;

Si merveilleuse, si forte, si belle, si odorante et rayonnante.

Sa chaleur est rassurante mais aussi effrayante.

Unique et délicate merveille,

Je voudrais qu'elle puisse rester éternellement.
Mais elle finira par s'affaiblir et s'éteindra.

Mais qu'a-t-elle besoin?
Qu'a-t-elle besoin?

Je crois qu'elle n'a besoin que de moi.

Liberté

L'écriture est libératrice!
Personne ne juge les peintures d'un artiste.
Personne ne condamne les couleurs et les formes à l'envers.
Personne ne juge la signification des pensées.
Vous êtes libre d'être tout ce que vous désirez.

Dear future self,

Thank you for your constant efforts to support this path and for never giving up on me. You finally pushed the doors of success. These wonders deep inside your heart are amazing. Intuition takes away the creator you are. This treasure influences your whole world. Ever since the spark ignited, you've been looking for something to do with it. May this gift change the world and inspire more than one. You will make your place as you have always wanted. You have probably already done so by the time you read these words.

Now is the time to write your next article, your next issue, your next novel, piece of heart and first bestseller. There is indeed a world out there eagerly awaiting your arrival.

Mel

About the author

Melissa Calixte is a writer, copywriter and fitness professional in Quebec, Canada. She promotes and raises awareness of self-discovery, passion, interests and self-realization. It is about true love and the power within. Her first published memoir: *Fire*, is born from this perspective. Passionate about writing, music, health and well-being, she lives in Montreal where she hopes to inspire her daughter and the young generation to become their best selves by showing them that anything is possible.

Made in the USA
Monee, IL
07 July 2026

56550983R00064